THE MINISTRY OF THE SACRISTAN

THE MINISTRY
OF THE
·SACRISTAN

PREPARING AND
MAINTAINING
THE LITURGICAL SPACE

Frank Winkels

THE LITURGICAL PRESS
Collegeville, Minnesota 56321

To
Gert Drinville

Cover design by Ann Blattner. Photo by James L. Shaffer.

2	3	4	5	6	7	8	9	10

Contents

Introduction

Have you ever visited another parish church? It is immediately apparent to anyone that there are varying degrees of care which go into the preparation of the worship space. Some are purposefully and meticulously laid out for celebrations. Others rely on chance to get the liturgy rolling! This small volume is intended to encourage a flexible structure for the work surrounding the physical preparation of liturgical space.

Preparation is the key to a prayerful celebration. If a parish is aware of this, they are also aware that other structures are in place to foster parish prayer. These include a parish council, a liturgy commission, various task-oriented committees, involved clergy and staff, and a well-developed music program. If the community does not already have a liturgist or liturgy coordinator, realize that such a person is an invaluable asset to unifying parish liturgies, and well worth the salary, whether full- or part-time, or as a combination liturgy/music minister.

Many liturgists will find this volume a handy reference for "brushing up." Other parish ministers, especially sacristans, will find help in improving the use of facilities and artifacts. This is not, however, primarily a "how-to" for decorators and environment crews, but an aid to the execution and maintenance plans and principles that the environmental people of the parish have set forth. The suggestions here are sometimes simple, sometimes more involved, and often given in a lighthearted vein so that we might not get caught in the trap of taking ourselves and our jobs too seriously.

No parish is perfect or ideal; neither does this modest manual presume to be. Local adaptation needs to be taken into consideration as well as the abilities and proclivities of parish personnel in order to bring about growthful liturgical change.

Valuable help in the organization of these ideas was given to me by Mr. Larry Reynolds. Mr. Robert Thompson of the Office of Worship of the Diocese of Kansas City, Missouri, and Mr. James Murray shared helpful liturgical insights as well.

May the liturgical prayer of the Church be deepened and heightened by the simple application of the principles contained here!

1

Basic Principles

It is important to know just what the role of the sacristan is, and how it interacts with the clergy, liturgist, liturgy committee, etc. The document of the Bishops' Committee on the Liturgy *Environment and Art in Catholic Worship* (1978) is, or should be, the guide for all of the aforementioned ministers. They will all be working toward the same goal if it is used well! Perhaps the old term "sacristan" is a bit limiting in terms of the duties today associated with the physical preparations for the liturgy, but it is a convenient one. Sometimes and in some places, certain aspects of the sacristan's role are assumed by the other ministers mentioned above.

The sacristan's role is to maintain the plans of the liturgical planning teams for the seasonal environment of the liturgical year, and to prepare the necessary furnishings, etc. for the various ministries. These include presider, deacon, servers, lectors, Communion ministers, hospitality ministers and crucifers, and occasionally the musicians (coordinated by the music director). Sacristans also oversee day-to-day maintenance of liturgical objects, and offer help in improving areas of the environment as necessary. (Sometimes this may mean taking the bull by the horns.)

It has been my experience that the best environmental situations are achieved after at least two to three years of careful, pre-meditated improvements. Don't try to improve everything immediately! Parishioners and ministers do not, as a rule, like the furniture rearranged all at once. Do, at least mentally, make a plan of what needs to be done in each area.

Perhaps the liturgy budget is not given a high priority in your parish. Your job, then, is to prepare, to the best of your creative ability, the liturgical space and whenever possible, raise awareness of the needs in this area. Perhaps your parish is so large that it is difficult to get parishioners involved. We need reminding that many folks have to be asked to help with these tasks. Some, perhaps, think that things at the parish happen by magic! When you see someone with a specific talent, make a note of it.

In terms of essential principles for the sacristan, three come to mind: simplicity, balance and respect. Simplicity means choosing to clarify clutter, using less instead of more, and heightening the symbols used. Complex artistic designs are fine, and sometimes necessary, but be careful in using too many, too close, too often. An analogy: chocolate ice cream, cole-slaw, vegetable soup and mashed potatoes are each delicious in their own right. What cook with full faculties would serve them all mixed together? In order to pray well, Catholics need the clarity to see into the depths of symbols. What you do matters greatly in achieving that goal. Small things and their use all add up!

Balance is another area which needs attention. People are more important than things; however, things reflect people's attitudes. Liturgy must be inviting. Therefore, the physical environment should be inviting, no matter what the style. Be careful not to confuse external piety and prayerfulness, for they are not the same. Fussy arrangements can easily become stiff and stand-offish, and can give the impression that people are not necessary to complete the ensemble. It is rather similar to a "stay-off-the grass" vs. a "come-to-our-lawn-party" mentality. When liturgical space becomes a fence which keeps people out, this balance certainly has not been achieved. This leads us to the third and perhaps most important consideration.

Respect for the assembled community is of primary importance. This does not mean fear of the assembly (just in case you are afraid of changing things). What it does mean is that the liturgical environment should be as carefully and beautifully prepared as available resources permit. An appropriate analogy might be that of the home dinner party. Would a good host and hostess allow the house to be a mess for such a gathering? Would the table be set with everyday linens and dishes? Would the meal be served with the television blaring? Would the hosts dress improperly? What about the community of Christians gathered for the ultimate feast?

The liturgical year and its feasts and seasons also demand our respect. If the environment gives off a scent of "business as usual," perhaps a little improvement is called for in adapting to each particular celebration. Liturgy is something people do, not something they watch. In order to speak deeply to humans who are by nature transitional, living in a cyclical world, the Church in wisdom gives us an ever-changing (and yet stable) liturgy which is not to be flattened out or homogenized into a "same-time-next-week" thing.

Respect the building in which you work. There are two common misunderstandings here, the first being the use of styles and colors which clash with the building. This is not to say that old and new cannot be mixed. But when doing so, there must be a unifying thread. The second misunderstanding often encountered is that of blindly maintaining the *status quo* with regard to objects and artifacts (which may or may not match the building). Worn-out or inappropriate things have no place in the liturgy. Such objects need to be reworked, renovated or replaced, upon consultation with qualified artists and craftspeople. To furnish improperly an otherwise beautiful building is indeed a tragedy.

Respect is due you in your role as a sacristan, and therefore a job description setting forth your responsibilities is called for. If there is not some such structure already in place, sit down with your supervisors to develop one so that expectations on both sides can be realistically met.

In this booklet these principles will be applied to each area of the environment of the worship space in greater detail, giving concrete examples for improving celebrations.

2

Vesture

Handling and laying out the vestments for the priest was the main duty of the old-time sacristan and it is a part of the current overall preparation. Given today's full cut of ministerial vesture, it is best that they be hung rather than laid out in drawers. Sacristans should know the components of liturgical vesture; they are briefly described here.

The alb (from the Latin for "white") is the white, floor-length garment which may be worn by all ministers who vest, up to and including the presider. In some places the lectors and cantors vest, but more commonly they do not. Altar servers should be cautioned to wear albs that are long enough; in many places, it seems the day in which they were measured for size is long past. It is easy to make albs for servers from kits or by scratch (if funds are short). Albs help to unify the appearance of the ministers; cassocks and surplices ("blacks and whites") do not. Red cassocks go a step further, calling undue attention to a secondary ministry by confusing red as liturgical color with red as everyday color.

Albs are worn primarily as a symbolic reminder of baptismal commitment and resurrection. Lightweight albs for the presider are always worn under other vestments and never alone (even in summer) as they are not sufficiently ample in cut nor elegant in appearance. In hot weather an amply-cut alb and stole are sufficient vesture for the presider at Mass.

It is also appropriate for other celebrations. Generally, avoid albs with colored or very lacy decoration. Plain is best.

Cinctures (cord belts with tassels) are normally used only by the priest if at all. They are sometimes used with servers' hooded albs to good effect, but should be white, brown or another neutral color.

The stole is used by the presider and deacon, the latter's crossing the body and connecting on the right side. Although it is necessary to keep them in good repair, do not use stole guards (basted-on cloth strips) at the neck as in years past. This is like keeping the plastic slipcovers on your furniture when company comes! If a stole is worn out, try to replace it. Stoles should be long enough to be dignified. Choose simple designs rather than those which are over-decorated. This will avoid a "billboard look." Cords, chains, tassels and trims for aesthetic or functional purposes are not problematic. For concelebration (more than one ordained minister at the altar), the outer vestments should match, including stoles. At the very least, the fabric textures should be similar, and the shades of colors should harmonize.

The chasuble is the large outer garment worn by the presider (usually not concelebrants), and the dalmatic is the sleeved corresponding vestment for the deacon—usually for special occasions. Both should be full-cut and long (almost floor-length), and not overly decorated. Stoles must match or coordinate. They are usually worn over the other vestments, especially if they are wide. Narrow stoles are meant to be worn under chasubles. Be careful to iron out any large or deep wrinkles in all vestments.

Copes are floor-length capes used for non-Eucharistic celebrations, such as anointing, Morning and Evening Prayer, Stations of the Cross, Palm Sunday, Good Friday and other processions, Benediction, and some weddings and funerals. Copes are useful and have authentic liturgical roots. However, they are often outmoded and dilapidated. New ones can be made quite easily, the most useful colors being, in order of importance and necessity, red, white and purple/blue. Enlist a local textile artist/sewer to make some. (Chasubles are actually only to be used for celebrating the Eucharist.)

A few general hints for making vestments are in order: (1) Resist the temptation to use garish or loud colors. Rich colors are often more harmonious with their surroundings. (2) Do not overdecorate, especially with crosses; let the shape, cut and color do the work. (3) Use fabric that breathes, and as a rule avoid heavy and/or stretchy knits. (4) Explore hand-woven fabrics, if possible. (5) Texture and quality speak louder than attached symbols.

The colors for liturgical use are: white for Christmas, Easter, the solemnities, etc.; purple for Lent and Advent, with blue being an as-yet unofficial option for Advent, and sometimes combined with purple; rose (not pink) as an option for a Sunday each in the middle of Advent and Lent; green for Ordinary Time; red for Passion Sunday, Good Friday, Pentecost, confirmation, etc. Blue is also sometimes used for Marian feasts, though unofficially. The small volume called the *Ordo* gives the colors and calendar for the entire liturgical year. It is the official book giving the order of the Church's prayer: Sunday and daily Eucharist and the Liturgy of the Hours. Every sacristy should have one handy.

Most priests do not ask that their vestments be laid out as in the past, but usually remove the appropriate vestments from hangers. Sometimes a special vestment stand is present for this use. It is courteous, though not necessary, to hang or lay out the clergy vesture for the day's celebration, especially if there is more than one set per color and only one is appropriate for the day. Many times a funeral set, for example, will match the pall (large cloth used to cover the casket) and should be given preference. The pall, when stored, should be folded as little as possible and laid in a drawer or hung on a padded bedspread hanger. Occasionally it should be pressed to remove large wrinkles. It is usual to fold it in thirds lengthwise and then in thirds the opposite way.

Store all vestments not in use in another location. Garment bags (cloth are best) come in handy. Group others according to color, putting the deacon's vestments in a separate cabinet if possible, the priest's stoles together, as well as the albs. Special stole hangers are available. Servers' albs should always be in a separate cabinet if possible. Avoid use of mothballs in cabinets. If a deodorizer seems necessary, launder the vestments more frequently. Carefully check the labels for care instructions. Albs will need the most care in all the typical places. Never use dirty vestments, for it is at least a venial sin!

It is not too much to expect the ministers, up to and including the presider, to hang up their vestments after the liturgy. Be especially scrupulous with the altar servers. They are capable of developing good habits. Soiled albs by the tens are not something you should be spending long hours on. Post a prominent reminder and sign it for best results (a kind word to the presider usually corrects any difficulty in that department).

3

Liturgical Objects

Familiarity with the objects needed for worship will aid the sacristan in the demystification of their use and maintenance. They may be broken down into a few main groups: books, vessels, things that burn, and sacred images. The next chapter will deal with liturgical furniture and other objects not specifically liturgical, but necessary for liturgy.

Books

There are several books the sacristan needs to be concerned with, the most important being those used by the ministers. They are (1) the Sacramentary, or book used at the altar; (2) the Lectionary, book of readings; and (3) the Gospel book, or Evangelary, containing only the Gospel readings. Be sure to store them in the right place so they may be found easily, keeping them clean and neat. Clips and loose papers should be removed. Ideally, the ribbon markers provided should be used and, if notes are necessary, they should be contained in a neat (preferably hard-cover) folder apart from the book. If the books have cloth or other covers, keep them clean and neat as well, always replacing tattered ones. Perhaps parish needlework artists can be enlisted to design and make attractive seasonal covers utilizing cross stitch, needlepoint, crewel, hardanger, or similar types of handiwork.

The dignity of God's Word demands that lectors reverently use the Lectionary to read from, never a missalette or loose sheets. On occasion (e.g., children's liturgies), readings may be proclaimed directly from a Bible, in which case it should be in excellent condition and preferably hard- or leather-bound. The physical sign of the book should be beautiful and clearly recognized as a symbol of the Word.

Congregational hymnals for the ministers are necessary for their full participation. A few copies should be labeled "sacristy" and stored there for the ministers' use. Also, the sacristan or another person or group should be responsible for the maintenance of the assembly's books, keeping them in good repair. Experience has shown that leaving a damaged book in the pew encourages others to play with undamaged books. The nonverbal message is given that it must be all right to do so. Monthly or seasonal missals, apart from liturgical shortcomings, are very difficult to maintain, and demand regular attention when they expire. It is worth the effort to explore the possibility of hard covers for them to keep them presentable. If your parish uses monthly missals or seasonal/weekly leaflets in combination with, or instead of, hymnals, make sure they are stored in the pew racks, or in stacks at the ends of pews in the absence of racks. This would be an excellent ongoing task for the ushers, greeters or a group of young people. The care of hymnboards is directly related to that of hymnals. Tidiness and thoughtful organization count here as well.

Lectors should cover all loose sheets needed for the liturgy, most preferably with a hard cover folder. A small "cheat sheet" for the presider—neatly lettered or calligraphed—may be laid by itself on the altar next to the corporal. It is inadvisable to keep books other than the Sacramentary on the altar, for it alone is proper to the altar. Normally, when a book is not in use, it is removed to the credence table, held in a minister's grasp, or returned to the sacristy.

Vessels

Vessels need not take up the sacristan's time as they once did, but they do need occasional attention. The chalice is a primary example of a liturgical vessel. Many are now made of stoneware, an easy-care material. Other materials make good chalices, as long as the material is non-porous, such as stone, wood, crystal, etc. as well as metals. Keep chalices very clean, and leave no residue of any kind inside or out. Except for pewter, metal chalices are almost always plated. Clean and polish them gently, as the plating is usually not thick. Use a soft cloth and good quality polish if necessary. Never use abrasives. Plates and *ciboria* (plural of *ciborium*, which contains the bread) are treated the same way, and are also often of stoneware. Use a damp purificator to wipe off any remaining bread dust. When setting up for liturgy, whoever is responsible should see that the vessels match or coordinate closely. Also, any metal vessels with chipped or corroded plating should either be replated or replaced.

Crumbs or hosts which are found after a liturgy or while cleaning should be reverently disposed of without being overly scrupulous. They may be rinsed down the *sacrarium*, a special sink in the sacristy which drains directly into the earth. Or they may be consumed if clean. Likewise, surplus consecrated wine must be consumed and not stored (hospitals being an exception) because of danger of spillage. For further information, see the Bishops' Committee on the Liturgy document called *This Holy and Living Sacrifice.*

Chalices are not draped with a veil (as in the old liturgy) so that the sign value of the cup may be seen as clearly as possible. The "chalice pall" (a hard, linen-covered board formerly used to cover the chalice) was originally used to keep insects out of the cup!

A number of other vessels are needed for liturgy. Cruets for water (A = aqua) and wine (V = vino) should be kept clean with regular rinsing, always being sure to use fresh water. The small *pyx*, used to carry the Eucharist to shut-ins, should be stored in a convenient place. If it has a cloth or leather cover, keep it in good condition. A wine flagon for Communion under both forms (increasingly common on a weekly basis) may be either of glass, stoneware or metal. The monstrance or *ostensorium* is used for occasional celebrations of Eucharistic adoration or Benediction of the Blessed Sacrament. When not in use, it should be kept covered to keep out dust, and stored in a safe place in the sacristy. Keep this vessel well polished.

Bowls of various kinds (usually of stoneware or glass) are needed. They include: the lavabo for the priest to wash his hands, a baptismal bowl for a temporary baptistry and dishes for ashes used in the distribution on Ash Wednesday. Be sure to keep all bowls emptied and clean after use. Glass is sometimes preferred since it allows each substance to be seen. Additionally, there may be a large pitcher and shell for use during baptisms. Any of these vessels need to be kept free of residue and spotlessly clean (would you wish to be baptized with anything less than that?). To remove any stubborn deposits from these objects, try using undiluted white vinegar on a cloth.

Things That Burn: Candles

The next category of liturgical objects includes those things which are burned (all creative liturgy people have a bit of the pyromaniac in them). Candles are perhaps the most regular component of this group. Of chief importance are the altar candles. There are usually only two candles at the altar, unless festival times of the year are being celebrated. Some sanctuaries are arranged with four candles (or torches) placed at the corners or steps surrounding the altar, and may be "stepped" or arranged together carefully for variety.

If a flower and candle arrangement is used, the candle might not be the pillar type but some other decorative form such as a votive or vigil light. Undue ostentation in this department usually proves to detract from rather than add to the overall effect.

Keep candle wicks trimmed to about a quarter-inch length. Do not allow them to fall into the molten wax when extinguished, for this will cause you nothing but grief later! Always use a properly-fitting "follower" (the brass or glass piece that goes on the top of the candle) as it will allow the candle to burn longer and more evenly with very little dripping. Only extremely large diameter candles do not need followers. At one time liturgical law prescribed that a certain amount of beeswax must be present in altar candles. Though that law is no longer on the books, candles with beeswax are a good idea. They burn well and long, and do not drip or smoke as much as high-paraffin content candles. They look good and are actually quite economical. Other materials can be considered, as long as they fulfill these requirements adequately.

As a last resort candles may be placed on the altar, but they must never obstruct the view of the action which takes place there. If they do, consider getting freestanding holders and placing them next to the altar. One such type of holder is called an altar or processional torch which consists of a floor receptacle, a metal or wood standard which is grasped when carried in procession, with a plate and candle socket on the top, made to fit an average-size altar candle. Many churches now use one or more pair of these torches. Those with a colored glass globe covering the candle should be avoided, as it does not allow the imagery of the candle itself to shine through. However, a simple clear glass shield could be used, thus saving carpet or floor and vestments from damage.

Similarly, avoid the "candle tube" or, worse yet, electric substitutes for candles. The burning down of a candle, besides being a rich and intriguing symbol of light, helps us mark time by its growing smaller and being replaced. Natural is always best.

The paschal or Easter candle is of singular importance as a symbol of light in many celebrations. It is to be displayed with prominence at funerals, baptisms, and the fifty-day season of Easter.

A few points need to be made about the Easter candle. It needs to be of commanding proportions, even in small worship spaces. There should be no visual confusion between its size and that of the other candles used at the altar or elsewhere. In order to be seen in procession or when on display, size (both height and diameter) is a primary consideration. Likewise, if the holder is not proportional, the whole works can easily look quite "spindly." Consider having a holder made or obtaining one if such is the case. Sometimes the old "bier lights" used at funerals in years past can yield a suitable holder, even if one needs to be refurbished or adapted.

Be sure to keep the wick and top of the candle very neatly trimmed so wax drips and soot are not allowed to spread. The decoration on Easter candles varies, but it is safe to say that as usual, less is more. Try to find a candle in which the design is integral, such as colored horizontal stripes, wax inlay, or perhaps the traditional wax nails and incense grains (usually explained in the package they come in), or some other type of "classy" and creative design. Avoid those with plastic decals. After all, you'll be staring at it for a whole year.

Above all, do not use a paschal candle more than one year! A new one is required to put across the Easter idea of newness of life in Christ, and the marking of liturgical time in the parish celebrations of baptism, burial, and seasons of the year. During the times the paschal candle is not specifically in use, it should be prominently displayed by the font/baptistry area, and not stored in the sacristy closet! Another idea concerning the use of this candle might center around the All Saints/All Souls celebrations. Beginning October 31 at the All Saints' Day vigil liturgy, place the Easter candle on its stand in the middle aisle (in "funeral position") along with a Book of Life to be displayed there throughout November (the Book of Life is a bound volume with blank pages, placed on a stand, perhaps with Scripture headings on each page, in which parishioners are invited to record the names of those beloved to them to be remembered in the Church's prayer during the month).

Concerning the lighting of altar and other candles, experience may show that altar servers, especially younger ones, do better with a book of matches than with the traditional long-handled candle lighter/snuffer. Unless a candle is out of reach, matches are neater, safer, and do not call attention to themselves. The wax tapers used in the lighter are often misused, and large flames sometimes threaten to ignite things they should not. Wax from them can drip and sputter, and soot from them can dirty the surroundings of the candle. This is especially true when lighting votive candles in arrangements: matches invariably are neater. Consider abandoning those long-handled contraptions; you'll not regret it (books of matches are also cheaper than boxes of lighting tapers). Retain one long-handled snuffer (minus the lighting taper) to extinguish the Easter candle, so as not to remove it from its holder while it has a pool of hot wax in the top. Many stories can undoubtedly be told of wax-covered cherubs' heads: servers who thought they should take the big candle down to put it out or move it before the wax was solid. As an alternative, a long-arm butane lighter may be the answer, since it is safe and inexpensive.

Beeswax candle stubs can be returned to the candle dealer for a rebate on the next candle purchase. As well as being an ecologically sound practice, it saves dollars for the parish. Label a box or drawer in the sacristy for this purpose.

The maintenance of votive candles or "vigil lights" used for personal devotion is often the duty of the environment/sacristy crew or sacristan. They should be kept clean and free of debris lest they crack. Shattering glass can be a real hazard with these candles. Cleaning large numbers of these candle glasses can be made easier with the use of inexpensive electric buffet warming trays upon which scores of spent glasses are heated. This makes the removal of the metal piece and residual wax much easier. An old cookie sheet (preferably a "jelly-roll" pan) in a 125 degree oven will also do nicely. *Never* use a microwave oven for this purpose, as it is extremely dangerous! Also be careful not to cut yourself on stubborn sharp metal pieces while trying to remove them. Always use a tool of some kind. As mentioned above, votive candles are sometimes used in arrangements at the altar to function as the altar candles. Whenever and wherever this type of candle is used, be sure not to leave the old metal piece from the spent candle in the glass when replacing with a new one. The new candle will be tilted, and the flame heating the glass will almost surely crack and break it. Messes and scenes of that nature are no fun!

The larger ten-hour votives are usually more practical for decorative purposes, since they do not need replacing as often as the smaller candles. Smaller candles for devotional purposes are more economical.

Never should these devotional lights compete with the liturgical space. If there are too many, consider reducing their number. The larger six-day or similar candles should be treated so as to minimize their confusion with the tabernacle or sanctuary light, the latter being visually considerably larger, and hopefully far enough removed from the votives. Remember: votive candles are always to be subservient to the liturgical celebration, since they are devotional in nature. They should be displayed at a place of veneration, such as the Mary and Joseph niche, and not by themselves. If there are stands full of votive lights alone, consider placing them together by an existing statue or painting so that the visual connection of veneration and remembrance of faithful departed is made. Keep the stands or holders clean and provide a small sand-filled dish in which to stick long wooden matches for lighting.

The tabernacle lamp should be, as mentioned above, distinctive by its size and location. Always keep it lit adjacent to the place of Eucharistic reservation. The glass container is sometimes covered with a glass globe (often, but not necessarily, red). There are wonderful so-called crackled glass globes available which are very distinctive in appearance. Keep the surrounding area of the light free from soot. An oil lamp would provide a distinctive source of light for the tabernacle area instead of a candle.

Things That Burn: Incense

The use of incense completes our pyrotechnical discussion. The incense thurible or censer is used at funerals as well as other solemn liturgies, especially in procession. The thurible needs to be kept in good condition. It has a chain or chains with a ring holder at the top from which it is swung. Be sure it is in good repair! The cup which contains the actual coals needs to be kept fairly free of debris--no easy task, you will find. Carefully scrape the interior free of large unburnt incense grains, and clean off the resin residue from the lid. Keep the outside clean. Also, inform the servers not to store the thurible too soon after a funeral or other celebration, or you will have a smoke-filled room when you least expect it! It is best to take it outside, empty it into a solid metal container (such as a coffee can) and hang it on its stand to completely cool.

Usually it is best to bring in the thurible only when needed. Try not to leave it hanging around the sanctuary in full view as it needlessly takes up space. Remember this rule of thumb: if something is not in use, take it out.

A brazier (stationary incense pot) is used quite often at evening prayer and other celebrations. It can be a large stoneware bowl filled with sand in which is placed the charcoal. Use a couple of charcoal disks in a brazier so the incense burns a little longer and denser. In a censer or thurible, one may be sufficient, unless you are incensing toward the end of the liturgy. Read the directions on the charcoal box carefully to figure out how to light the pieces. It is not all that difficult, but can be startling the first time it sizzles and sparks.

The incense boat is any small attractive container with the incense grains in it, including a small spoon for the presider, deacon or server to sprinkle the grains onto the burning coals. If yours is a tarnished metal example, either replate or replace it, perhaps with a small stoneware dish (which may match better anyway). Check the boat(s) periodically to make sure that you in fact have the goods at the proper time. Some parishes keep more than one kind of incense on hand for variety, though that can be an expensive habit. Again, richness of symbol is important. The presider should use plenty of smoke so that there is a real connection with the senses (not just a going through the motions).

The celebrations during which incense may be most effective should be similar to this list: the entire Christmas season, especially Epiphany, Ash Wednesday, and the Sundays in Lent (in the opening procession only), Holy Thursday (in closing procession), Good Friday (at the Intercessions), the Vigil and Sundays of Easter, Ascension, Pentecost, Corpus Christi, Marian feastdays, All Saints' Day, and the parish patronal feast.

Sacred Images

Other liturgical objects requiring only occasional attention from the sacristy crew are as follows: (1) crosses, both stationary and processional; (2) icons and statues; and (3) the tabernacle for the reserved Eucharist. Stationary crosses, including the Stations of the Cross, should be occasionally dusted or polished if possible. Processional crosses should be kept in good repair. See that they are perfectly straight when planted in their holders. Where there is a large crucifix in the sanctuary, it is best not to display the processional cross as well, especially if the processional cross also has a corpus (the representation of Jesus' body). After the processional (during which the cross is carried by the cross bearer), it is taken to the sacristy or a hidden alcove in the sanctuary. More than one cross usually visually diminishes attention rather than intensifies it (see *Environment and Art in Catholic Worship*, no. 86). Do not leave the processional cross out if not used for processions, especially if it is in the same area as another stationary cross. Try putting it away and see if anyone notices!

Covering crosses and statues during Lent is no longer accepted practice. Drapes added to but not covering them can, however, be quite effective. Adding a Lenten cross in the sanctuary is fine, but then be sure that other crosses and crucifixes are either removed or completely concealed so as not to divide attention.

Statues, icons, and paintings should be kept dust-free and in excellent condition. Do be careful when cleaning around works of art. Also, keep in mind that multiple images of the same saint in the same space is very much discouraged. Let the primary image (e.g., of Mary) speak for itself, and do not unduly decorate it or place another, similar image near it. Purity in this area really pays off because imagery is clearer and nothing is placed in competition with the truly liturgical nature and use of the worship space.

Likewise, the tabernacle is an area which should be kept free of attachments. One sanctuary light is to be kept lit nearby (except during the triduum of the Paschal season—after Holy Thursday liturgy and during Good Friday and Holy Saturday when the light is either put out or removed entirely, the tabernacle being left open). Lacy altar cloths, too many flowers and candles, art work, frilly tabernacle veils, etc. would not be dignified and fitting anywhere in the worship space regardless of style, but least of all at the tabernacle and surrounding area. Simple seasonal hangings or tapestries are an effective alternative. In addition, the tabernacle is to be placed in a specially reserved area to the side of the sanctuary if not in a separate chapel. It is not to be in a central or prominent area. The altar and pulpit/ambo alone are to be the primary points of focus during Eucharistic celebrations.

If your tabernacle space falls into the above category, fret not—but do gradually try to bring out the simplicity of the symbol of the reserved Eucharist by un-decorating the area. You are actually emphasizing its importance in so doing, and not degrading it in any way. Be careful not to change everything at once, unless you are prepared to handle a considerable amount of ire on the part of at least a few parishioners, and do so only with the backing of the liturgical committee, pastor, and liturgist. Timing is everything.

4

Furniture

The four main liturgical furnishings/areas in any Catholic church are: altar, pulpit or ambo, font, and chair. God is present in each community primarily in the people gathered in the Lord's name. They are led by ordained ministers who often function at the chair. God is present in the Eucharist and baptism (altar and font), and is surely present in the Word (pulpit), the story of our salvation. Therefore, it is very important that the physical symbols be strong and clear for the community to relate to them visually.

The following should be on the altar and, except for the cloths, only at the Preparation of the Gifts: a cloth or cloths (perhaps seasonal in character), usually a corporal (though some churches do not use them if the cloth is sufficient), the Sacramentary, chalice, paten with bread, and a purificator. Sometimes two candles are placed on the altar. If possible, the priest's microphone should not be placed there unless it is very inconspicuous. This precludes the use of a large and visually cumbersome microphone stand. According to the Sacramentary, it is not necessary to place a crucifix *on* the altar. Almost always, there is one nearby. A missal stand or pillow should only be used if the priest is visually impaired. Objects such as these serve only to convert the altar into a "liturgical coffee table."

Under no circumstances is it a good idea to use plastic coverings on the altar cloth during the liturgy with the idea of preventing spills of wax and wine. A gracious host never leaves the plastic slipcovers on home furnishings.

Side altars are sometimes present in older worship spaces, at one time being used for "simultaneous Masses." If this is the case with your building, (un-)decorate them in such a way that they are not visually confused with the main altar. This would mean that any cloth placed on them would not be ornate. Any flowers present would be simple in nature, and any art be noble and modest. Lit candles are not placed on side altars, especially during the celebration of Mass, lest they detract from the central action at the altar. Even if the tabernacle rests on a side altar, the tabernacle light should be the only candle near it.

The pulpit or ambo should be used to proclaim all three readings. A separate lectern can be used by the cantor for the leading of assembly singing. Any seasonal decoration which is hung on the pulpit should match or coordinate with that of the altar as closely as possible. A separate small lectern should not be used for the first and second readings. This sends a clear message to the assembly that those readings aren't as important as the priest's. Surely the first and second lessons, as well as the psalm, are as closely related to the feast and season as the gospel. As in the case of the altar, the pulpit should not be used as a liturgical end table. When the readings and Prayers of the Faithful (if they are read from here rather than the cantor's stand) are concluded, the lector removes the books and folders.

Baptismal fonts and baptistry areas are treated differently from place to place, but wherever they are located, certain guidelines should be followed. First, the font and surrounding area should be kept very clean. Fonts and temporary baptismal bowls (for baptisms occasionally held away from the baptistry) can be cleansed of stubborn residue with the ever-popular and inexpensive white vinegar. Most often, water with a little detergent will do the job. If you have a large immersion font, such as that installed in all newer worship spaces, do not put detergent in it if there is a fountain mechanism. This could create a most unfortunate situation, if not an entertaining one. A small fishbowl strainer can be used to remove an occasional stray particle in a font with non-moving water, but regular changing of the water to keep it fresh is a more thorough solution.

Usually a small table or shelf is needed on which to place the necessary liturgical accoutrements for the baptismal celebration. Often there are green plants and/or flowers by the baptistry. It is imperative that they be kept in A-1 condition. Dead or semi-alive "living" things do not send good vibrations to the assembly concerning the spiritual powers of baptism. Neither do stainless-steel holy water "samovar" dispensers placed in church entrances. For those desiring it, baptismal water may be obtained from the font itself.

Likewise, the presider's *aspergillem*, or water sprinkler, and boat need to be clean and free of mineral deposits. Plastic water bottles for sprinkling, for example, do not speak positively to the assembly as a baptismal reminder.

Sometimes a shell is used to pour the water on the head of the infant. It is more common than not to find these in poor condition, especially those of brass. It is fairly inexpensive to replate such a shell (perhaps in silver instead of brass if that color works better), or have a vacationing parishioner pick up a real scallop shell of large size (also very inexpensive) in Florida or Hawaii. Remember: natural and authentic objects are almost always better, both in traditional and contemporary environments.

For temporary baptismal bowls, use a stoneware or glass bowl of ample size (similar to a large punch bowl) with no decoration, or with simple liturgical artistry. Many potters will make one of excellent quality for a nominal fee. A permanent baptistry is the ideal.

Related to the baptismal font are the holy water fonts. If your space has them, it is imperative that they be very clean and free of mineral deposits, and without sponges. The strength of the sign depends on the water's clarity and depth. Fill the fonts so that fingers dipped there get wet!

The "presidential chair" is the large chair for the presiding priest at the liturgy. Its placement should be such that it does not appear like a throne, yet clearly in a leadership position. The gathering or introductory rites of the Eucharist are led from here, as well as other parts of the liturgy. Altar servers' chairs are usually best in another location so that the servers do not give the visual impression of being "little priests." Clearly, the lector(s) and cantor have a primary role to play in the dialogue of the liturgy, and they often sit in the assembly as part of it and not next to the presider. The servers' main purpose is to help prepare the space and assist the presider by holding books and other objects. When they are not doing these things, they should be seated away from "center stage." On the other hand, the deacon (when present) should sit next to the presider.

Without getting into the issues concerning the design, function, and placement of liturgical furnishings, there should be very few if any barriers between the ministers (presider, cantor, lector, servers, etc.) and the assembly. This includes Communion railings, even in buildings registered on historic preservation lists. Inclusion on such a list does not prevent communities from making necessary renovations for their use. Many parishes realize this and have removed railings and other such barriers including unnecessary pieces of furniture such as kneelers, chairs, and unused tables. If furnishings are not being used, store them out of the sanctuary.

When tables, chairs, stools, kneelers and so on are really necessary, be sure that they match both in color and style. Do not under any circumstances use folding tables and chairs for any sanctuary function; they are neither dignified nor appropriate. It is possible to have older wooden objects refinished so that unity of color can prevail in the furnishings. All upholstered objects need to match as well. Too many colors in both types of objects usually account for the visual confusion sometimes found in parish worship spaces. Upholstery should lean toward the natural and not possess even a hint of glitz. Kneelers for weddings are sometimes upholstered with needlepoint art. Care should be taken that the design not be gaudy in nature.

The credence table or shelf holds the necessary objects for the day's liturgy and is located in the sanctuary away from the altar. Such objects include the lavabo bowl, pitcher and towel, water cruet and books and vessels not in use. A simple white cloth may be placed upon it, but the credence should not look like a small side altar. The gift table is placed in the rear of the church, and on it are laid only the single large plate (paten) with bread, and the cruet or flagon of wine. Simple seasonal decoration which remains on the gift table is also appropriate.

Care in choosing the type of candlestick or torch is also important. Do not mix styles of furnishings without careful thought. Usually, it is best to find objects that really fit the architecture of the building. It is unbecoming to place modern objects in a traditional space, and vice versa, but there are notable exceptions to this rule. For example, sometimes a pair of large and ornate gold-plated candlesticks (originally for high-altar use) can make wonderful altar torches in a newly-renovated or even an ultra-modern building. Trust your instincts: if it looks wrong, it probably is!

Flags are often a problem for the sacristan. Without appearing unpatriotic or disloyal to the Vatican, it is wise not to place flags in, or even near, the sanctuary. They should be off to the side if they are present at all. Certainly, the worship space is just that, and Catholics definitely need to have environments which clearly direct their hearts and minds to the business at hand, not to symbols of secular or even Church institutions (see *Environment and Art in Catholic Worship*, no. 101).

Plant stands are often a source of visual confusion. Whether of wood, metal or another material, they all need to match! Music stands should also blend in with the environment to avoid a visual sea of black created by a large number of them in one place. Try spraying them with a neutral color to match the wall or floor, using appliance paint for a long-lasting finish. It is worth the effort.

Furnishings often do not seem like they make much difference in the function of the environment. But taken together they may create either a functional unity or a disjointed conglomeration. By removing, rearranging, refurbishing, or replacing some or all of these pieces, a more hospitable space for the parish's worship is created.

5

Building Features and Their Maintenance

Perhaps this chapter is better directed toward the parish custodian, but often the sacristan and crew will be at least peripherally involved in the scheduling and execution of these activities, so they are included here.

Lighting helps create a hospitable atmosphere, but it is necessary that whatever the lighting system that it work properly, right down to the last bulb. Check the fixtures periodically. Sound equipment is often the province of the music director, but sacristans should be conscious of where the equipment is stored, keeping a close eye on its condition and presence. If there is a tape recorder/deck connected to the sound system for recording weddings and other celebrations, it is a good idea to keep a couple of extra blank recording tapes handy for emergencies.

Carpeting in worship spaces is, in most cases, limited—and with good acoustical reason. However, the sanctuary and/or aisles are often carpeted. It is handy to keep some Carpet Fresh available for accidents (which always occur when you don't have any). To take demon candle wax out of carpeting (or linens), try a warm iron and a piece of paper bag (not newspaper) to blot it up. Chewing gum should be removed by rubbing with an ice cube which will harden it so that it can be scraped, the remainder being removed with Goof-Off or other spot remover. Floors need to be kept clean to give a welcoming appearance to parishioners and visitors. Schedule the waxing of floors (which inevitably comes before Christmas and Holy Week) to avoid conflicting with rehearsals, reconciliation, putting up the Christmas decor, etc. Nerves will be saved as a result, not to mention your faith (pastors tend to be happier, too).

Stained glass and other windows should be kept clean, at least as far as possible. Often they are out of reach, but periodically they and the rest of the building should be professionally cleaned if necessary. Walls can be a problem to clean. Consult a painter or decorator for detailed help. Pews and bookracks should be kept in good repair and occasionally cleaned with Murphy's Oil Soap. Consider making some pew ropes for use at small-group celebrations to keep the assembly seated together, especially at funerals. It is really hospitable to minimize unused pews so that the parishioners sit close behind the family and other mourners. When making ropes, use a good grade of soft-finished, twisted nylon cable, premeasured. Install connectors on the back pews and on the pews where the ropes will end. (These ropes are equally useful for wedding gatherings.)

Also important is the exterior appearance of the building, especially the landscaping. At the very least, it should be picked up and carefully mowed, with shrubbery neatly manicured. If your talents lean in the direction of design, don't be afraid to share your ideas with the powers-that-be.

Keep the entrances free of debris, giving them a "once-over" after Saturday weddings and before the weekend liturgies get underway. Keep bulletin boards current. In order to put forth an inclusive, hospitable public image, pamphlet racks should be monitored by the parish staff for stray materials. If missalettes and hymnals are stored in entryways, they need to be kept neatly stacked and maintained. Throw away old bulletins and newsletters. Cluttered vestibules do not give a good first impression to people entering the building. Presumably, environmental design people should not neglect these areas as suitable for seasonal decoration (see *Environment and Art in Catholic Worship*, nos. 54, 103), as they are the first contact worshippers have with the liturgical space.

6

Flowers and Plants

One of the chief duties of the sacristan is to maintain and often to arrange the flowers and plants used in liturgical decor. By far the most important rule of thumb in this area is that "less is more."

Floral Arrangements

Often, one well-planned and executed arrangement at the altar or in the sanctuary is far better than more than one haphazard or mediocre bouquet. Unless the style of architecture is extremely symmetrical (same on both the left and right sides), asymetrical arrangements to one side or the other are many times more visually pleasing, as they create a dynamic balance between the objects and furnishings. When arranging and placing flowers and plants, remember that the main variable is missing from the sanctuary and assembly space: the people, who are the moving scenery. Never obstruct sight lines or access to any place by improper placement of an arrangement.

Do not neglect flowers and plants in other places: pulpit/ambo, font, perhaps the tabernacle and the assembly space as well. Sometimes sanctuary or other steps provide a built-in vertical grade which can be used to good advantage when grouping many potted plants and flowers. If the altar torches have their own movable holders, try using them on steps with one wonderful flower or plant arrangement to create an organic whole (remind the servers to be careful when placing the torches in their holders during the procession so as not to damage themselves or the arrangement). The torches need not be extremely close to the altar to function as altar candles. Arrangements likewise need not be on or near a wall. They are often more attractive and dynamic when freestanding.

It is not necessary—nay, it is often undesirable—to have two matching sanctuary bouquets: one on the left, one on the right. Quite regularly one sees such arrangements for weddings and funerals, the remains of which (no pun intended) can be very troublesome to deal with. Perhaps your parish has its fair share of such celebrations weekly, and you are to make sense out of the arrangements which are left over. The proper use of what are often good materials can be a real savings for the parish over having to purchase flowers for the weekend liturgies. Be not afraid to haul the leftover bouquets into the sacristy for a little "surgery." Take them apart, select a suitable container for the new arrangement, and get to work.

Keep in mind some basic principles for flower arranging: stability (both physical and visual), dynamics, unity, texture, and color. First, the arrangement has to stand up! It has to physically fit into the space for which you need it (most beginners err on the side of making things too small). Choose flowers of the proper height for the kind of arrangement you are creating. Choose a basic shape to stay with, then start filling in the main components, using frogs or florist foam if necessary. Perhaps you could group together the various kinds of flowers and greens at your disposal on the countertop for quick visual reference. Don't use too many textures, colors and types, but select materials which will best convey the season and feast being celebrated. Give away your leftovers to innocent bystanders to take to their families, shut-ins, etc.

A dynamic shape for an arrangement (e.g., a left or right sweep, a globe shape, a long narrow bunch, etc.) often gives it character. Do not mimic a florist who churns out endless arrangements for weddings and funerals, creating cloned collections of generic-looking specimens, all in a triangular shape! Be original and creative, using the gifts God gave you. Once again, however, less is more.

If you are so inclined, buy a good book on the subject or take a class in floral arranging, for the information contained here cannot possibly do more than touch on such an engaging part of your work as a sacristan. Skill in arranging really can only come after much practice.

Floral arrangements are not to be placed directly on the altar. Obstruction of the liturgical action by a part of the environment is definitely to be avoided. As mentioned before, the only things that are placed on the altar are the elements (bread and wine), vessels, cloth, book, and maybe the candles.

Floral Maintenance

Maintaining cut flower arrangements is not all that difficult, except perhaps for roses. Keep bouquets filled with fresh water if possible. Be sure to check them as they arrive at church for funerals and weddings. Often florists do not water them for fear they will tip in transit. Water them immediately. Roses will droop easily from lack of moisture and/or excessive heat. They sometimes need to have aspirin or another additive put in their water to help preserve them. It is also helpful to make a fresh cut on the stems so they can get the nourishment they need. Remove immediately any arrangement which shows signs of waning.

After floral bouquets have outlived their usefulness, be certain to glean from them such usable "permanent" flowers for drying as baby's-breath, statis, and heather for use in certain types of arrangements and for making permanent wreaths for entrances, etc.

Christmas trees also need to be meticulously watered in order to keep their needles—no danger of overwatering here.

If your church uses artificial trees at Christmas for practical reasons (sometimes directly at odds with good liturgical reasoning), threaten to hold your breath indefinitely until "they" have a change of heart. Real trees are better.

Potted plants and flowers are not as easy to maintain as cut flowers. Do not, above all, overwater, for the damage overwatering creates is far more difficult to correct than that caused by underwatering. Yellowing, mushy leaves, and other maladies are usually traceable to too many sacristans each giving every plant "just a little drink." Choose one person to do the watering. Sometimes plants need to be moved during the week to get enough sunlight if the worship space itself is not well-lit. Find a safe spot for "intensive care," possibly with gro-lites, and stick with it. The following is a table for pinpointing plant troubles and correcting them:

Mushy yellow leaves, soft stems, soggy soil:
Too much water.
Drain if necessary, and pray it lives.

Dry brown or yellow leaves, edges curled:
Too little water and perhaps too much heat. Drench plant to revive, and thereafter water regularly. Misting may also be called for.

Pale leaves, small or spindly new growth, weak stems:
Too little light. Move to bright spot until needed in church.

Leaf tips of ferns turn brown:
Use scissors to cut bruised leaves. Try to locate where people will not brush against it.

No new growth:
Perhaps needs to be fertilized.

Sudden dropping of leaves:
Sudden rise/fall in temperature. Move it away from drafts, etc.

Plant is crowded or root-bound, and wilts easily:
Needs to be repotted.

Plant has insect pests:
Wash thoroughly, and consult a florist.

Consult a florist for more information on any plant-related malady. Do not wait until it is too late!

Propriety

Concerning vases and containers, be certain that they coordinate with the environment. Good quality stoneware, glass, wood, etc. is preferable to plastic or the white papier-mâché florist containers. Local potters can often come up with wonderful vases of large size (often hard to find in stores) and good design for a very reasonable cost. For potted plants, always remove the ribbons, bows, and foil and cover the pot with a wicker basket or something similar. A selection of baskets and unglazed clay pots should be kept on hand. Be very careful of "cute" effects; they often lead to an eyesore in an otherwise meticulous decor. Foil, if used at all, needs to match from plant to plant. More than one color is undesirable and calls attention to itself. Many wonderful arrangements are ruined because of an incongruous coupling with a poorly-chosen vase or container.

No good reason exists to use plastic, silk, or other artificial flowers or plants. No area of the world (except maybe Antarctica) is without natural vegetation suitable for liturgical use. If a parish uses plastic plants or the like anywhere in the worship space, the very first duty of a conscientious sacristan would be to raise the parish's awareness to the necessity of using authentic living things in the worship of the Church. Ultimately, the imitations should be disposed of. The richness that real blossoms and greenery bring and the lifeless and ill effects of using synthetic imitations are two concepts of which the sacristan needs to be very conscious.

Flowers obtained commercially need not always be a part of good arrangements. In the midwestern states, for example, a typical autumn bouquet might be: long-stemmed pampas grass, thin cattails sprayed with hairspray to fix, colored leaves, bittersweet, or a branch full of high bush cranberries, wild purple lithium or black-eyed Susans and some brilliant crimson sumac leaves with seed pods left attached, and perhaps some dried milkweed pods, Japanese lanterns, or dill flowers.

Last, be careful not to use flowers except in a very limited way during the penitential season of Lent. It is important to convey a sense of stripped-down, stark simplicity in preparation for the festive season of Easter (see the *Introduction to the Roman Missal*). This includes St. Patrick's Day and St. Joseph's Day, should they happen to fall during Lent (which they almost always do).

7

Linens

Liturgical linens occupy a great deal of sacristans' time. These fabrics are divided into two groups: large and small. Here we will deal with their construction, care, and storage.

Actually, the only component of the large cloth category is what is known as an altar cloth. These fabrics are not always constructed of linen, and so the term "linens" is used quite loosely. The fiber content of altar cloths and all liturgical textiles varies greatly, though linen probably still occupies primacy of place in the greater scheme of things.

The construction of altar cloths depends upon the altar, the parish, the season being celebrated, and the degree of solemnity desired. The simplest example is a plain white cloth which merely covers the *mensa*, or altar top, without hanging over. The next example is a dignified, simple piece which covers the *mensa* and hangs nearly to the floor on the left and right side (or front and rear). Another type often used (sometimes not to a very graceful advantage) resembles a table cloth such as would be found in the home. It hangs over all four edges, but only slightly (maybe 6–8 in.), giving the appearance of the old "frontal." For more solemn/festive occasions, many parishes have made cloths which hang to the floor on all four sides with fitted or rounded full corners. Dubbed the "Laudian or Jacobean cloth," it is quite popular in England.

Overlays that resemble table runners, in a color scheme that harmonizes with the season and feast, are sometimes placed in fairly narrow strips, or singly over the regular altar cloth, running either from front to back, left to right, or one or more of each. Referred to as *antependia* (singular: *antependium*), these overlays need to harmonize closely with the other colors and textures used in the building, especially with ministerial vesture! (Tutti-frutti color schemes, I repeat, do more to add to a disorganized atmosphere than probably any other problem.)

Construction of altar cloths should follow these guidelines: (1) select a fairly easy-care fabric, but one with some texture (not necessarily white, but a solid subtle color); (2) determine how the cloth will be used, selecting one of the styles above; (3) calculate the amount of fabric needed through careful measurement; (4) buy more than you need and wash the cloth to preshrink it; (5) construct the cloth with careful attention to the dimensions of the altar (recheck by laying the pieces on top of the altar, pinned together if necessary, before sewing); (6) hem by hand, if necessary, for a good finish, or carefully hem the edges, making sure that they will endure repeated launderings.

Storage of altar cloths should be in drawers, laid out, or rolled onto a large tube rather than folded and hung on hangers which tends to crease fabrics. Group by color and type, and fold them as little as possible, thus saving on additional work. When ironing altar cloths, try pressing the cloth on the altar itself with a steam iron using a long extension cord. A professional steamer works well also. Fold up the edges of the cloth and press them first. Iron the top last. The front of the cloth is the most crucial part, so step back a distance (with the room lights on) to see whether you have missed any spots while pressing. (Do not iron directly on a wooden altar.)

Small altar linens are of many varieties. The following need to be present in one form or another in every sacristy: corporals, purificators, lavabo (hand) towels, and baptismal towels. They all need to be of a sufficiently absorbent cloth.

(Ever wonder why linen really caught on? That's why.) Corporals range from the old square cloths to larger ones up to 24 x 36 in., a preferred range of size. Some parishes do not use them at all, especially where the altar vesture is deemed very sufficient. Corporals may or may not have a small red cross embroidered in the center (the cross is handy on larger corporals so that the middle point may be found). Corporals were historically used to determine what elements were deemed consecrated and what were unconsecrated. Today, their use is more of a practical consideration. They protect the altar cloth by making the cleaning of spills and crumbs easier. Corporals should not be creased as in times past, for they should lie flat. Large corporals, especially, should not be folded, but laid flat in large drawers.

Purificators are the most necessary small liturgical linen used. They should be kept clean and thrown in the hamper at least every other day if not after every liturgy. Purificators are not as large as corporals, and are always creased in thirds, the right side folded in, then the left on top. An additional crease is then added in the opposite direction to form an "M" shape, the middle of which is smaller than the ends, allowing the corporal to be hung over the top of the chalice, if desired. If your parish distributes Communion under both forms (bread and wine), it is necessary to have a good supply of purificators on hand, all in good repair and all matching. As with corporals, there is usually a small red cross embroidered in the middle of the white cloth, but certainly not always. Hems should be very neat. Corporals and purificators can be easily made, and if you have a good supply of old amices (a part of the old collection of priestly vestments no longer used on a wide scale), they may be cut up to make altar linens without spending lots of money to purchase cloth. If you do need to buy fabric to make linens, be careful of some synthetics which do not absorb moisture well. Never use stained linens.

Lavabo towels are used by the presider to dry his hands

at the Preparation of the Gifts. Many places use a good white terry-cloth towel, which is perfectly acceptable. Others use linen, which, though absorbent, wrinkles very easily and can look quite shabby after one use. One square yard of terry-cloth will yield at least four good sized lavabo towels if you need to make them. Towels may be colored, but are often white.

Baptismal towels are small cloths, perhaps half the size of a purificator, used to wipe the head of the baby at the font (I prefer terry-cloth rather than scratchy and stiff linen. Undoubtedly if babies could talk, they would too, so there is no need to keep these special cloths on hand). Use a regular lavabo towel for infant baptisms and a larger white terry-cloth towel for an adult.

Caring for altar linens poses no great difficulty. Though anyone can learn to do so, perhaps one person in the parish should be entrusted with that task alone so that they are prepared consistently. Starch is not a part of that preparation. Indeed, fabric softener is a better idea! Spray-N-Wash or a similar spot remover may be needed from time to time on a stubborn red-wine stain. But other than that, regular laundering is not much different than usual. Steam irons on damp linens help get out deepset wrinkles, so it is best to remove them from the dryer before they are completely done.

Be especially good to those persons who take care of the altar linens: they are saving you a lot of work, and the parish a lot of money!

8

Setting Up for Liturgy

The liturgical year is a cyclical celebration of our salvation in the Lord. Yet sacristans sometimes do not see it as such. Instead, it seems like a never-ending onslaught of liturgies which leaves barely time enough to gasp for breath before beginning anew. Prior planning for the celebrations (presumably done in large part by the parish liturgical planning committees) tends to minimize these feelings, and can put one in a much more pleasant frame of mind. Perhaps the following "Ten P's for Public Performance" (originally written for musicians) might help to keep the whole issue in perspective: Proper prior planning plus practice positively prevents poor public performance. If a few basic principles for the seasons are kept in mind and a checklist for celebrations becomes a habit, liturgies will tend to run smoothly.

Advent-Christmas

The Advent-Christmas season is often troublesome. Keep in mind that flowers during Advent should be simple. The solemnity of the Immaculate Conception is still part of the season, remember! Plan the decoration of the creche or nativity scene carefully, avoiding any "cute" effects. Advent wreathes, which many, if not most, parishes use during the season in various forms, need to be kept fresh. Greens may need to be replaced sometime during the season. Be sure that a new set of Advent candles is used each year. The burning of the candles represents a marking of time, and that sign is not clear unless they are new to begin with.

It is not a good idea, incidentally, to place a creche scene beneath the altar, unless absolutely no other location is available. The altar, as mentioned before, needs to be kept free of attachments so that the Eucharistic sacrifice is as clear as possible. Be sure to keep all trees well watered during Christmas. Don't let the environment fade after Christmas Day. Plan to carry the environment through to the Baptism of the Lord, but not beyond that. Poinsettias have no place beyond a few weeks after the season is ended because of their seasonal connotation. Change their containers, group them differently, etc. to give a clear impression that the season is completely over (I recall one parish which kept their poinsettias alive and kicking well into Lent).

Ordinary Time (Winter)

This season should be fairly simple. If you are responsible for flowers, try making a winter arrangement of birch branches, cones, berries, evergreens, crabapple branches, or perhaps bittersweet, instead of a floral arrangement. After the garland comes down from Christmas, you may find a few unwanted deposits of resin where they don't belong. Use a little paint or lacquer thinner (or Goof-Off) to remove them.

Lent and the Triduum

When Ash Wednesday rolls around, be sure to find the can of palm ashes which you saved from last year's palms. Check to see how many distribution stations there are to be at the liturgies. Take some shallow dishes (perhaps stoneware, made just for this purpose) and put a small amount on each one. Not much is needed to "smear" a great number of people. *No* flowers during Lent! In the environment for Lent, occasionally dried or non-floral arrangements have a place, but really nothing else. As a sign that baptism does not take place until Easter, and as a sign of desert-preparation of the community, perhaps empty the baptismal font and the holy water fonts at the entrances, and maybe even fill them with sand! Powerful signs indeed, but be sure to educate people as to the whys and wherefores. Lent is a good time to thoroughly clean the building, if schedules permit.

For Passion/Palm Sunday, take the palms (stored upon their arrival in a cool place to prevent shrivelling), and divide them into groups, one for each entrance, reserving more for the main entrances. Arrange the palm bunches neatly on tables draped with red cloths or some other classy arrangement and, if necessary, place a small, neatly-lettered sign thereon asking parishioners to take a palm on the way in, or giving some other direction. When greeters hand out palms, a sign is superfluous. If your parish owns a red cope, it should be used for the beginning of today's celebration. Fan palms can be used for decoration as well.

Each parish's observance of Holy Week is unique, so only general comments will be made here concerning these most holy days of the calendar. A parish's finest is always to be brought out during this week. These special celebrations are absolutely central to the observance of the liturgical year. On Holy Thursday have available a pitcher, basin and large towels if the rite of foot-washing is to be observed. The place of Eucharistic reposition should be in another room, if feasible. When it is necessary to place it in the assembly space, it should not be near the sanctuary. Because the New Passover is not completed, it is important to represent this idea in a visible way by keeping the Eucharist in a separate location. Avoid at all costs any fussy effects to "make Jesus' home nice." After all, the mood of this celebration is somewhat somber. Sanctuary decor is to be as simple as possible, but flowers tastefully arranged in moderation are certainly desirable. Clean the thurible as well, for it will get quite a workout during this rite! Prepare the best incense and get the coals ready.

After the liturgy, the altar is to be stripped if the servers have not already done so. For Good Friday, prepare one large cross for veneration as per the instructions of the liturgical committee. Purificators for wiping it may be necessary, but somehow they don't give a very good impression. Consider an alternative way of veneration, such as reverently touching the cross with one's hand or bowing before it. Again, the red cope should be used for this, and for the celebration of solemn Stations of the Cross, if this is the parish custom.

Get a good night's sleep, because tomorrow (Holy Saturday) you're going to need it. Start early enough to maintain steady nerves. This most certainly goes for the environment crew as well on this most busy day of the year. Treat yourself royally and enjoy the preparations! Get the paschal candle ready and placed in the entrance, the plants prepared in baskets or other containers (remember: preferably not glitsy foils), the best altar cloth and *antependia* ironed, the baptistry cleaned and scrubbed thoroughly, congregation candles set in pews (if they are allowed), branches wired and taped together for the asperges (sprinkling rite) and the pyrotechnical department (thurible and candles as well as the bonfire) ready. The place really needs to put its best foot forward both for the beginning and the duration of the fifty days of Easter. For the Easter Vigil itself, a sacristan is usually a good choice to run the lights and the tower bells, so make that known to the liturgist if necessary—they usually appreciate it! On big days of celebration keep in mind that it looks gauche to use stubby remains of altar candles. Splurge! Bring out the expensive stuff!

Easter is finished on the Monday after, right? Wrong! It lasts up to, and including, Pentecost Sunday. Some places even prolong festivity through the feast of Corpus Christi, two weeks later. Be absolutely certain that the flowers, plants and greenery remain as wonderful as they were on Easter Sunday. It does not speak well of the resurrection that many parishes allow a gradual death to set in among the flora, culminating in removal of the corpses of formerly gorgeous blooms a short time after the First Sunday of Easter. In fact, plants and flowers should be replaced immediately when they begin to show signs of waning. If this means budgeting a smaller sum for Easter Sunday, in order to have more for use during the season, then do so! The results are well worth the effort. There can be fewer flowers as the season goes on, perhaps, but the feeling of festivity must be crystal clear.

Ordinary Time (Summer)

This season should be characterized by simplicity. Spring and summer flowers and plants from the garden can often be worked into the environment with wonderful results. If you are responsible for choosing vestments, do not overlook the green set just because it is "not a very important season." Every parish should invest in, or make up themselves, a simple but elegant set of green vesture for Ordinary Time. Consider using a different, darker green for winter to differentiate from summer.

Don't be afraid to rearrange the sanctuary furniture slightly for this season to break up visual boredom, thus helping to enliven the summer celebrations. Perhaps as fall sets in the environment crew will decide to opt for some fall colors. The selection of a dark hunter green for textiles may harmonize better with such a scheme. All Saints' Day in November beckons us to "pull out all the stops" (see chapter 3 for information about the paschal candle).

Baptism

For baptisms certain set-up procedures should be followed: the paschal candle be lit; the shell (if customary) and a soft lavabo towel be in place; the baptismal candles unwrapped, the baptismal garments (usually supplied by the parish) readied; the rite book for the priest or deacon and participation booklets for the assembly set out. If necessary, a pitcher of hot water to combine with the water in the font should be handy.

Confirmation

Procedures not normally followed sometimes mysteriously surface at the time of the bishop's arrival for confirmation. Good all-around parish liturgy should be the rule of thumb all of the time! The only special things required for confirmation surround the rite of anointing with chrism. Have a beautiful small dish cleaned and ready (similar or the same as those used for the ashes in Lent) into which the oil is poured. Buy a large, fresh lemon and cut it in half for the bishop to cleanse his fingers.

The Eucharist

The most celebrated sacrament, the Eucharist, is usually the one to be glossed over in our preparations. Consider celebrating the Mass with Communion under both forms if it is not done so at least occasionally already. To set up for this use matching chalices and purificators as well as plates, all placed on the credence table in the sanctuary, along with the water cruet. The flagon of wine and large plate of bread are placed on the gift table in the rear. Incidentally, the ratio of cups to bread distributors is customarily two to one, allowing the distribution of Communion to be accomplished smoothly.

Reconciliation

Reconciliation, held in a reconciliation room rather than a confessional, should have an inviting atmosphere, not dark or gloomy. The penitent needs a feeling of being welcomed back with open arms, so the room should be lit in a somewhat sub-dued fashion, spanking clean, with certain objects present and accounted for. These include a kneeler/screen unit for those wishing to remain anonymous, two matching chairs (one for the penitent, one for the priest), a Bible in good condition, preferably hard- or leather-bound, a large candle (lit for the celebration), a beautiful purple stole (not a leftover one), and a crucifix which is either freestanding, on a table, or wall-mounted. If there are too many crucifixes in the assembly space, one of them could well be moved into the reconciliation room, especially if the cross is of a smaller size. One parish had a wonderful Oberammergau cross hung at a side altar, originally used as a mission cross. A matching walnut floor stand was made for it, since it was about four feet tall, and it was placed in the rather large reconciliation room. Parishioners commented that it looked as though it had been made especially for its new setting.

Weddings

For weddings the set-up can be vastly different from place to place and celebration to celebration. The one thing to keep in mind is that normal rules of simplicity and liturgical propriety apply here as in all other parish liturgies. Seasonal decor, for example, should definitely be left intact for weddings, and not taken down or cluttered up. Either two chairs or kneelers are provided for the bride and groom, with the attendants seated in the assembly space for the Liturgy of the Word and the Liturgy of the Eucharist.

The lighting of the unity candle (a custom which shows little sign of dying out) involves limited preparation, requiring two tapers for lighting. Suggest using beeswax candles if possible, since they do not drip as easily nor burn as fast. The wedding candle itself will probably need a large-diameter holder. It is not a bad idea to keep one or two large wedding candles on hand for emergencies. Choose simple, not gaudy, specimens. Always light the wedding candle and burn it for a short while to start the wick prior to the wedding. This will save the couple from an embarrassing moment, should Murphy's law be activated during the candlelighting.

Place the three wedding candles anywhere away from the altar, preferably at the Holy Family or Mary/Joseph images. If they are to remain on the altar, remove any other candles. For easy cleanup, place a small cloth under them to catch drips. Blessed water may be used in the blessing of rings. A marriage rite book will be needed by the presiding priest, and perhaps a small "cheat sheet," or markers, in order to locate all the chosen options. If the bride and groom will be kneeling, the kneelers or prie-dieu, should not be draped. Programs and/or hymnals are to be provided for them as honored guests of the assembly (brides and grooms are certainly not to be spectators at their own wedding). Large candelabra (florist type, with many so-called "dripless" candles which usually aren't) should be discouraged. If they are used, they should be moderate in number, and non-centrally located. A clear piece of plexiglas, or similar square, might be placed beneath them to catch drips. Glass globes will accomplish the same thing. Likewise, "pew lanterns" should be even more strongly discouraged for the damage and clutter they cause.

After weddings, be certain the room is presentable for the weekend liturgies. All too often it may look as though a hurricane has just passed through. Check everything including sanctuary, pews, reconciliation room, entrances, bride's room, etc. If a disposable wedding carpet has been used, save it for making cleaning cloths (unless it is very dirty).

Funeral Liturgy

For funerals the paschal candle should stand in the middle aisle, and the pall should be folded and draped over a (back) pew.

The processional cross (if it isn't already used regularly), the thurible, and the baptismal water *(aspergillem)* should be ready for use. The Easter candle is often carried in the procession. Strongly encourage funeral directors to avoid bringing more than two or three bouquets into the assembly space. Ask the pastor to inform them of this policy. Check the pall periodically for large creases and iron if necessary.

Liturgy of the Hours

The Liturgy of the Hours—Morning Praise and Evensong— usually requires the Easter candle to be present, as well as a reading stand, suitably decorated, front and center. For Evening Prayer, a stationary brazier for the incense is needed (normally a stoneware bowl filled with sand and placed on a beautiful stand).

Feast Days

Special feast days, in particular those of Mary, may be treated in special ways! Perhaps a parish icon could be displayed in the middle aisle with a small arrangement surrounding it, possibly containing candles. There are many different ways to handle such celebrations.

Far from being complete, this chapter should serve as a springboard for your memory and imagination, assuring that proper prior planning is exercised in the celebration of the Church's liturgical life.

9

The Sacristy

Sacristies tell a great deal about a particular parish's celebrations. Correlations sometimes can be drawn between neat and well-planned sacristies and the beauty of the local liturgy (and vice versa, to be sure). The old adage "a place for everything and everything in its place" really has some merit. Most sacristans realize the value in neat working areas, the greatest dividend of which is the ease with which the various ministers can easily locate needed materials, sometimes at crucial moments. Therefore, it is a good idea to regularly conduct a cleanup patrol of this central ministerial convergence area: the parish sacristy. Do not leave messes lying about, but always hang things up and put things away, etc., generally tidying as you would your own home.

Undoubtedly many parishes already have a great deal of the necessary implements for sacristy work of various kinds. However, experience shows that often when one looks for a specialized tool for a specialized job, it may not be in its proper niche. Therefore, it is useful to conduct an inventory periodically to make sure the needed accoutrements are present and accounted for. The following is a list of items for a well-equipped sacristy:

vacuum cleaner and attachments (especially a crevice tool)

dust buster and bags
dustcloths and cleaning cloths
handbroom/brush

brooms
dustpans
wastebaskets
sponges
cleaning brushes for hands
dirty linen hamper
paper and plastic bags
hand towels
vestments, linens, and liturgical objects as mentioned in text

butter knife, paring knife, Xacto knife, large "art" knife (retractable)
nail clippers
flower clippers
scissors
hammer and nails
tacks (carpet and thumb)
screw drivers (large and small, and a Phillips)
flashlight (one that works, and also possibly a penlight for the Easter Vigil)
scratch paper/note pads
pencils (sharp) and pens
pins (straight, hat and safety)
needles and assorted threads
string (light and heavy)
paper clips
tag board
felt tip markers (permanent, fine point and italic)
easels for posters
stick-on labels
a labelmaker and tape
"reserved" signs

bulletin board with ministerial schedules (current) posted thereon
combs and hair brush
labeled lighting panel and sound system
floor-length mirror
paper cups
Kleenex
telephone book(s)
phone numbers (posted) for custodian, pastor, liturgist, sacristan
"lost and found" box
scotch, masking, florist, electrical, 2-way carpet and duct tapes
blank cassette tapes
extra 9-volt batteries for cordless microphone
steam iron(s)
extension cords (long and short)
matches (book and/or wooden)
warming trays (for cleaning votive lights)
charcoal
incense
altar bread
altar wine (possibly kept in a wooden case)
candles (altar, paschal, votive, Advent, tabernacle/ sanctuary light)
votive glasses in the proper colors
window and tile cleaners

Murphy's Oil Soap

wood polish, including Old Gold

white vinegar

fishbowl strainer for font

2 yds. clear hose for siphoning font

funnel

spot remover, such as Goof-Off

hangers, including stole hangers

lint remover

brass polish

Elmer's regular and wood glues

tray to drain cruets

tongs for charcoal

spoons for ashes and incense

first aid kit

extra Bandaids

smelling salts

watering cans with long spouts and large capacity

plant food(s)

plant trays to catch water

florist wire, foam, tape and spikes

frogs for arranging

vases (small, medium and large)

books (see p. 63)

regular and liturgical calendars

hymnals

A sacristan's job description is also included here as an example of what might be considered realistic expectations of such a position:

Job Description for the Voluntary Sacristan and Sacristy Crew

Objectives: The ministry of sacristan provides a vital service to the community. The sacristan does all those things necessary to keep the sanctuary and sacristy clean and orderly.

Each liturgy should take place in a space carefully prepared by someone who takes seriously the importance of the relationship between the faith and actions of a worshipping community and the appearance of the place where they pray.

Duties:

1) Provide the necessary time to clean and coordinate all vestments, vessels, decor, sanctuary, etc. by:
   a) sending items to cleaners
   b) mending
   c) washing items that can be laundered
   d) using one's initiative to get things done
   e) being conscious of small details
   f) maintaining floral and green arrangements
2) Oversee the care of all liturgical things by ordering wine, bread, candles, incense, charcoal, and all necessary supplies for liturgy

Skills:

1) Knowledge of liturgical terms and documents
2) Communication with liturgist and pastor
3) Knowledge of where supplies are to be stored and from where they may be ordered

Length of commitment: Twelve months

Training:

1) Any available workshop sponsored by the diocese
2) Help and support of parish liturgist and resources
3) Information in *The Ministry of the Sacristan*

Supervisor: Parish liturgist (or pastor)

Support: Parish liturgy committee, liturgist, friends, family

Evaluation: After every liturgical cycle

10

Conclusion

The parish sacristan/sacristy crew really has in its power the ability to enliven the parish worship by the proper visual and physical preparation of the space. It can be a thankless job, but a most necessary behind-the-scenes occupation which needs to be taken seriously nonetheless.

Regular meetings, at least yearly, of the entire sacristy crew or altar guild tend to create a good sense of camaraderie which can make the tasks at hand much more enjoyable. For the large jobs such as a thorough cleaning or rearranging of the sacristy or worship space, be sure to thank the workers by taking the time to prepare a small treat and coffee, or some other snack. Coming together for such times are real opportunities for Christian fellowship, combining both "Mary" and "Martha" aspects. Be conscious of that, and do not be afraid of doing a little educating about liturgy when the occasion arises (without, of course, becoming too preachy).

Posting a prayer and providing each person involved with a copy is another way of saying that what we are doing is important to the community's celebrations. It is appropriate to close this booklet with a pair of invocations of blessing on this ministry:

Give blessing, O God, Creator of the Universe,
on this house of celebration.

May it be for all of our parishioners who will gather here
not just a place of solace and rest, but also one of challenge.

Give the ministers of this community who serve herein
firmness of purpose to carry out your Son's gospel command
   to preach, feed, heal, anoint, forgive, baptize and bless.

And finally, give me, O God, heartfelt joy as I go about my
   tasks
together with those around me in the preparation of this space
for the ongoing worship of this parish,
as I realize the coming of your kingdom here on earth. Amen.

* * *

May these "Martha's tasks" be pleasing to you, Lord Jesus,
as I prepare this space for the worship of this community.

Let me put on a "Mary attitude," being ever glad to be in your
presence in these small jobs which ready us for celebration.

Help me to keep in mind the gospel values of simplicity and
hospitality so that this house of your people may be a sign of
openness and welcome to those who need the comfort and challenge of your message of love.

Blessed be your Holy Name. Amen.

References

The following books are part of a well-equipped sacristy:

Book of Gospels of the Roman Missal. 1970, NCCB.
Catholic Source Book, 1981, Peter Klein.
Documents on the Liturgy: 1963–1979: Conciliar, Papal, and Curial Texts. Collegeville: The Liturgical Press, 1982.
Environment and Art in Catholic Worship, 1978, BCL.
Lectionary for Mass of the Roman Missal, 1970, NCCB.
Liturgical Music Today, 1982, BCL.
Liturgy of the Hours, 1976, ICEL.
Music in Catholic Worship, 1983, BCL.
New American Bible, 1970, CCD.
Ordo, published each year.
Pastoral Care of the Sick, 1983, ICEL.
Rite of Baptism for Children, 1970, ICEL.
Rite of Christian Initiation of Adults, 1985, ICEL/BCL.
Rite of Funerals, 1971, BCL.
Rite of Marriage, 1970, ICEL.
Rite of Penance, 1975, ICEL.
Sacramentary of the Roman Missal, 1985, ICEL.
The Liturgy Documents. Chicago: Liturgy Training Publications, 1985.
This Holy and Living Sacrifice, 1984, BCL.

ICEL = International Commission on English in the Liturgy; BCL = Bishops' Committee on the Liturgy; CCD = Confraternity of Christian Doctrine; NCCB = National Council of Catholic Bishops.

These books are available from publishers and are sold at Catholic religious goods outlets and bookstores.